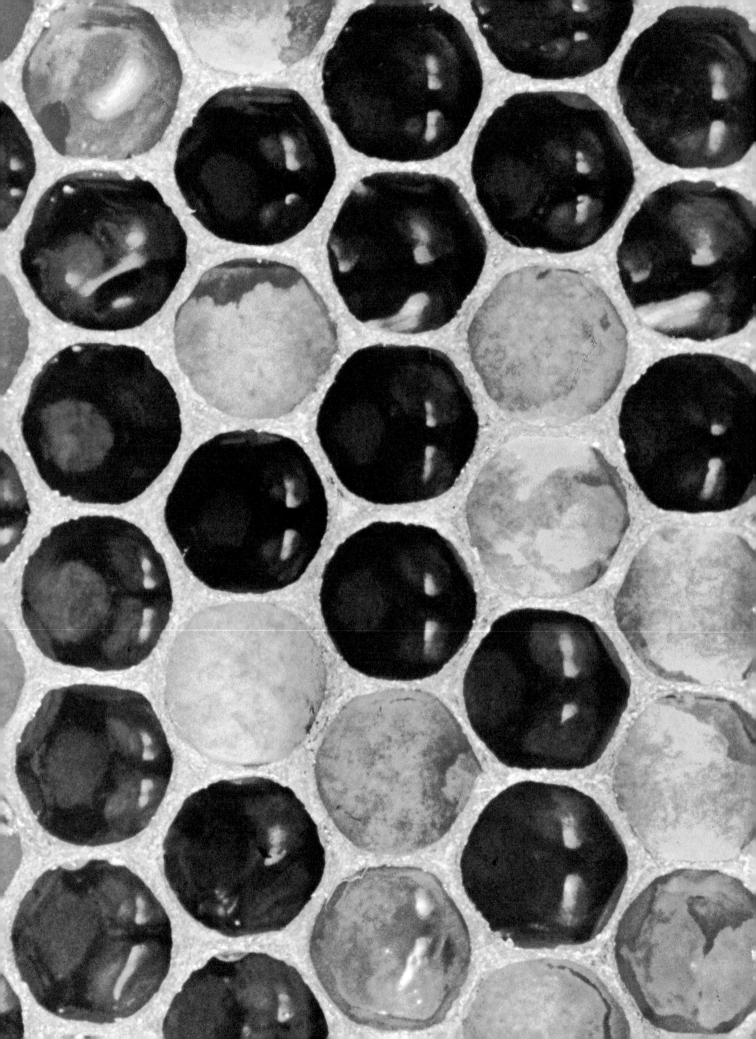

Honeybees

By Jane Lecht

☐ BOOKS FOR YOUNG EXPLORERS
☐ NATIONAL GEOGRAPHIC SOCIETY

BZZZzz

ZZZ! A honeybee flies low,
looking for food. She finds her way
to the flowers by following their sweet smell.
Then she zooms in for a landing on a pink petal.

Deep in the flower, the bee finds sweet drops of nectar. With her long tongue she sips the flower juice and carries it to the hive in her special honey stomach. Yellow flower dust, called pollen, sticks to her fuzzy body. The honeybee brushes the pollen grains onto the long hairs on her hind legs. Bees work hard gathering nectar and pollen.

Loaded with nectar and pollen from flowers, the honeybee heads straight home — in a beeline. The sun guides the honeybee to places near home. She steers toward the hive by remembering how far to the left or right of the sun she must fly. Then, she recognizes the plants and trees near the hive.

8

BZZzzzzz

Back in the hive, the bee dances to tell the others where she has found food. In one dance she buzzes and wags her body as she circles to form a figure eight. In bee language, her movements show which way to fly and how far to go. Over and over she dances. She stops only to let the bees smell the pollen and taste the nectar. Soon many of the bees will fly out to the flowers.

Thousands of bees live together in a hive.
Bees build honeycombs inside
their home out of wax. Here wax
oozes from a bee's underside.
Bees chew and pat the wax
into rows of tiny rooms,
called cells, that fit together.
Each comb has hundreds of cells
to store food or cradle baby bees.

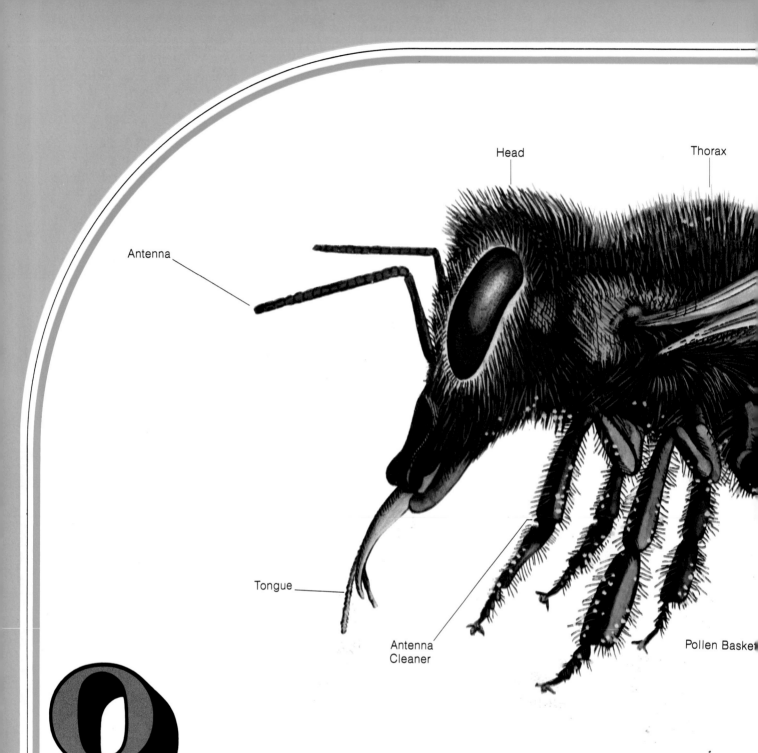

Head

Thorax

Antenna

Tongue

Antenna
Cleaner

Pollen Basket

Only a half inch long, the worker bee is the insect
that gathers nectar to make the honey we eat.
She has six legs, four wings, and two antennae.
She lives in a very large family, or colony,
with thousands of sister workers, a few hundred brothers,
called drones, and one mother bee—the queen.

Abdomen

Stinger

Pollen Brush

Queen

Drone

Worker

The queen of the colony
has only one big job—to lay eggs.
She lays only one egg in a cell.
A queen hatches upside down.
Two new queens fight until one is left.
There can be only one queen to a hive.
Workers always gather around the queen
to feed her and clean her.

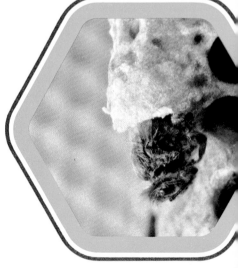

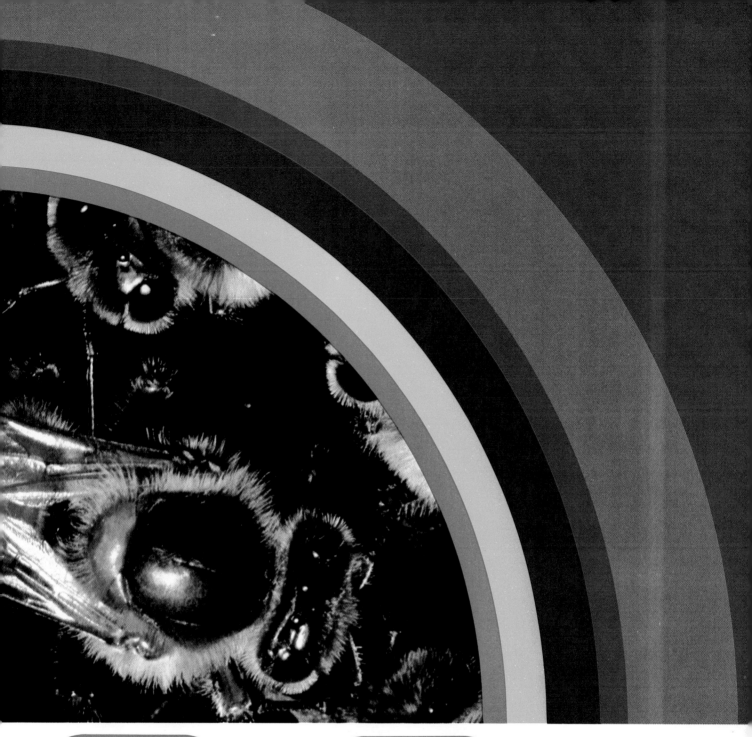

Each egg is shaped like a grain of rice. It hatches into a wormlike larva, which grows quickly. The larva turns into a pupa, and step by step it takes the shape of a bee. Two full-grown honeybees, a worker and a drone, chew the lids off their cells. They are ready to join the life of the colony.

Workers have many different chores in the hive. A bee pushes her tongue into a sister's mouth to take her load of nectar. She stores it in cells where it ripens into thick, sweet honey. One bee is poking her head into a cell to lick it clean. The next feeds a white larva. Two bees fan their wings to cool the hive. Guard bees attack a stranger to keep him out of the hive.

Drones have big eyes to help them find the queen as she flies above the treetops. Drones have only one lifework — to mate with the queen. They have an easy life and must be fed by their sisters.
In winter, when the food becomes scarce, workers push the drones out of the hive.

Enemies attack bees in the hive and field.
A green praying mantis has caught a meal.
A yellow spider has trapped a bee, too.
Bears love honey and will rob the hive.
Sometimes man is an enemy. When he sprays poison
to kill harmful insects, he also kills bees.

Under a microscope, a stinger shows its spiky barbs. The stinger comes out of the worker's body when she wants to defend herself. After she uses her stinger, the bee usually dies.

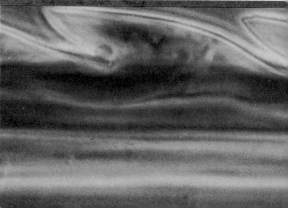

Beekeepers carry
wooden hives
filled with bees to fields
where flowers bloom.
These man-made hives
have rows of frames inside.
The bees build honeycombs
in these frames. Beekeepers
lift the frames out
to harvest the honey.
Bees sting only when angry,
but, just to be safe,
beekeepers cover their faces.

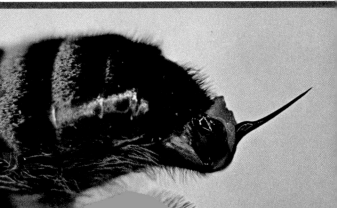

Combs hanging in the hive hold delicious honey. Honey comes in many flower flavors, such as clover and apple blossom. Because beeswax burns slowly and gives off a pleasant smell, it makes fine candles. Beeswax is also used in gum, inks, lipsticks, and crayons.

Bees and flowers are partners;
they need each other. As bees gather food
they carry pollen from flower to flower.
The plant needs pollen to make seeds.
Without bees many fruits and flowers would disappear.

You can safely watch bees behind glass at a nature center. Or you can visit a beekeeper. Or you can enjoy honey on bread. You can also watch the busy bees as they fly from flower to flower. Listen to the buzzing as they find the flowers with sweet nectar.

Prepared by the Special Publications Division of the National Geographic Society
Melvin M. Payne, President; Melville Bell Grosvenor, Editor-in-Chief; Gilbert M. Grosvenor, Editor.

Illustrations Credits

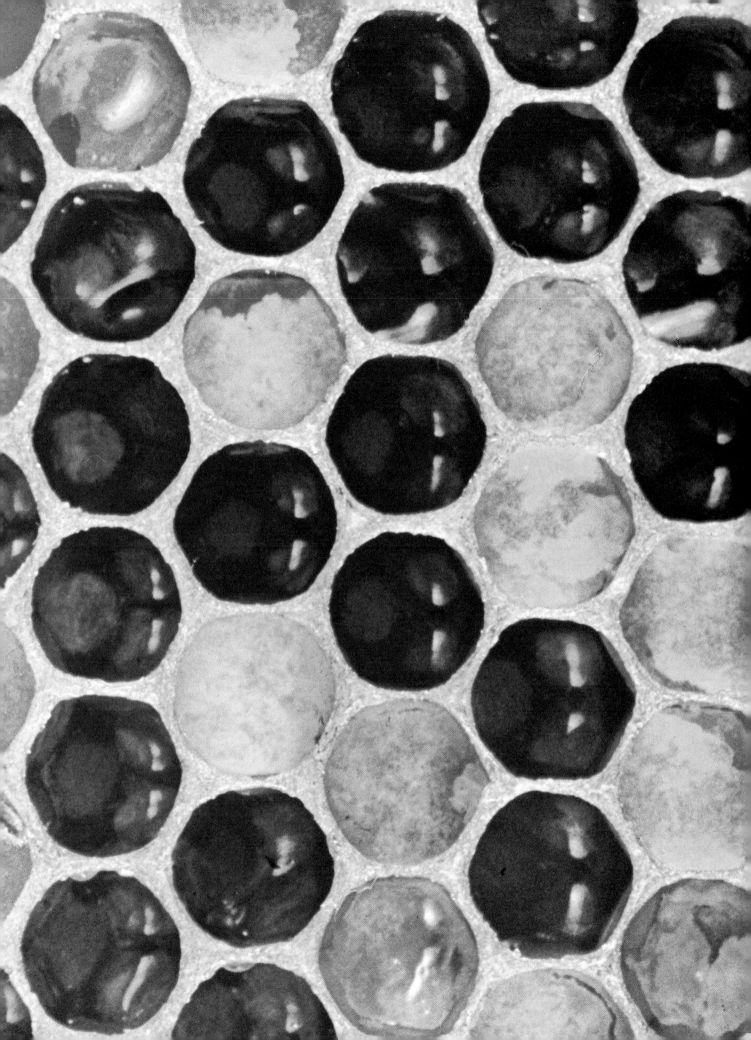